Adventure SPORTS

CANOEING and Kayaking

Stephanie Turnbull

A+

Smart Apple Media

Published by Smart Apple Media, an imprint of Black Rabbit Books
P.O. Box 3263, Mankato, Minnesota, 56002
www.blackrabbitbooks.com

Printed in the United States of America, at Corporate Graphics
in North Mankato, Minnesota.

Designed and illustrated by Guy Callaby
Edited by Mary-Jane Wilkins

Cataloging-in-Publication Data is available from
the Library of Congress

ISBN 978-1-62588-382-7

Photo acknowledgements
t = top, b = bottom, l = left, r = right, c = center
page 1 marekuliasz; 2t Oleg Zabielin, b objectsforall; 3 Andrew
Orlemann; 4 Ivan Chudakov; 5t evronphoto, b Ivan Chudakov;
6 O`lympus; 7 Yauhen Buzuk; 8t coxy58, b Ahturner; 9 Valeria73;
10 Richard Thornton; 11 Lane V. Erickson; 12t Steve Heap,
b Nelson Hale; 13 Baciu; 14 Ivan Chudakov; 15 LeonP;
16t Andrei Medvedev, c ap_i, r Sander van der Werf,
b Alan Gordine; 17 kaband; 18 Iakov Filimonov;
19 Maridav; 20 Kuznetcov_Konstantin;
21 BarryTuck; 22 Pri Ma; 23t Mark Yuill,
b LesPalenik/all Shutterstock
Cover Ivan Chudakov/Shutterstock

DAD0063a
052016
9 8 7 6 5 4 3 2

CONTENTS

FEEL THE THRILL

Think you have the skill, strength, and stamina to try canoeing or kayaking? If you'd like to try shooting through churning waves and risky rapids at high speed, read on...

Take the challenge

Imagine the excitement of whizzing down a fast-flowing river on a crazy adventure ride, paddling skillfully around jagged rocks and swirling whirlpools, before plunging over a waterfall in a cloud of spray. Canoeing and kayaking are seriously extreme sports!

*You need great control to steer a kayak through **white water** like this.*

Imagine launching your kayak over the top of a waterfall like this skilled paddler!

Tough stuff

Don't even think of riding waves or fighting strong **currents** without good training and plenty of practice. You must be physically fit to stay in control of your boat and have nerves of steel to deal with difficult situations.

 EXTREME BUT TRUE Whitewater rivers are graded 1 to 6 depending on how tough they are. Grade 6 is so dangerous your life may be at risk.

KNOW YOUR BOATS

Canoes and kayaks are both small boats in which you face forward to paddle, but there are key differences between them.

Kayaks

Kayaks are lightweight, usually made of plastic, and shaped to slice smoothly through water. A cover called a spraydeck keeps you dry. It can be removed quickly using a release tag, so you don't get trapped in the boat if you **capsize**.

spraydeck

seat

end grab

paddle

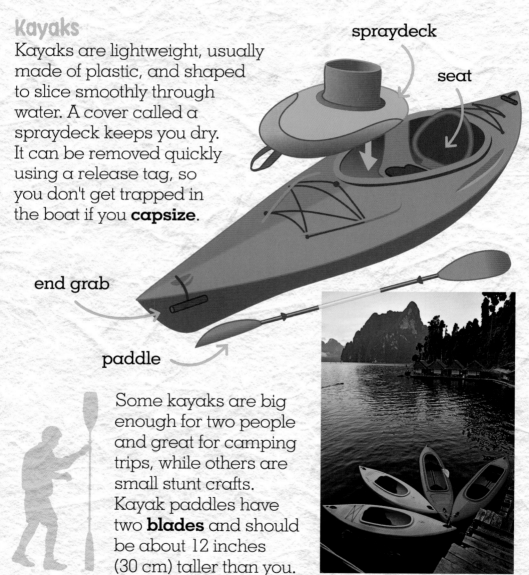

Some kayaks are big enough for two people and great for camping trips, while others are small stunt crafts. Kayak paddles have two **blades** and should be about 12 inches (30 cm) taller than you.

seat

seat

Canoes

Canoes are simple, open boats with space for camping gear. Paddles have just one blade and should come up to your chin.

*Wide canoes like these are very stable. Those with narrower **hulls** move faster, but are hard to turn.*

paddle

EXTREME BUT TRUE The oldest canoe ever found is around 10,000 years old. It came from the Netherlands and was made from a tree trunk.

Learning to canoe or kayak is fun. Join a club or take classes, and start on an indoor pool, slow-moving river, or lake. Always have an expert with you to help.

A group of kayakers learn essential skills on a wide, flat lake. They wear bright colors to be seen.

What to wear

Two essential safety items are a helmet to protect your head if you hit rocks and a flotation vest in case you fall in the water. Wear shorts and a T-shirt on hot days, or thermal layers and a waterproof rain jacket when it's cold. Some people wear a wetsuit.

Climb aboard

Learning to get in the boat can be tricky!
Start from a river bank. Hold the boat steady
with one hand and the bank with the other.

● *Kayak: swing one leg in, move
forward, pull in other leg, sit down.
Put feet against footrest, bend legs,
brace knees against the sides. Lay paddle
across boat. Fix spraydeck in place.*

● *Canoe: place paddle across boat,
step in, sit or kneel (kneeling gives better
control and allows stronger strokes). Keep
back straight; brace knees against sides.*

EXTREME BUT TRUE You should be able to swim at least 165 feet (50m) in your clothes before learning to kayak or canoe.

Sit up straight to stay
steady and don't
lean toward either
side of the boat.

PADDLING

Once you're in the boat, the challenge is to stay upright and move it where you want it to go! Here are some hints.

A kayaker pushes steadily and smoothly into deeper water using his paddle.

Ready and steady

Balancing in a narrow boat can be awkward at first, so it helps to be on calm water. When you feel steady, it's time to start paddling.

Kayak strokes

In a kayak, reach forward to paddle. Keep the paddle close to the boat, sticking up in the air. Use your body to push forward. To stop, put a blade in the water at about 90° to the boat. You'll feel the water press against it. Put the other blade in the water to slow down more.

In a large, open canoe, you may have people to help you paddle!

Canoe moves

Hold a canoe paddle with one hand at the top and the other on the **shaft**, level with the edge of the boat. Keep it as close to the boat as possible, paddling on both sides to go in a straight line.

EXTREME BUT TRUE Paddling at sea is extra hard because strong winds can easily sweep you away from the shore.

THRILL SEEKER

Helen Skelton (Britain)

FEAT
Longest ever solo kayaking river journey: over 2,010 miles (3,200 km)

WHERE AND WHEN
Amazon River, Brazil, 2010

You're sure to capsize at some point, so learn how to roll upright or escape from an overturned boat. You need to master these essential skills before tackling rapids.

Capsizing in fast-moving water can be extremely dangerous without proper training.

EXTREME BUT TRUE

Capsizing at sea can leave you cold and shivering. You need to find land fast, or risk **hypothermia**.

On a roll

When you capsize, don't panic. Take a deep breath and lean forward under the water, holding the paddle alongside the boat.

Quickly move the paddle blade across your body and up on to the surface of the water.

Use your body and the paddle to push the boat upright.

Practice these moves in calm water, near the shore, and with a qualified instructor.

Escape moves

If you can't roll, get out of the boat fast. In a kayak, pull the spraydeck release tag, push yourself out, then swim to the surface. In a canoe, either jump out before the boat capsizes or wait until you're underwater (so you aren't hit by the boat as it overturns) then push out and swim up.

WILD WATER

Once you're confident, you can hit the rapids—but don't take on more than you can handle. Stay in a group and stick with experts who can help if you get into trouble.

THRILL SEEKERS

Chris Spelius and Ken Lagergren (U.S.)

FEAT
First to kayak the Niagara Gorge, one of the hardest grade 6 rapids; hazards include a whirlpool 492 feet (150m) deep

WHERE AND WHEN
Niagara, North America, 1978

Start with low-grade rapids and gradually build up your skills and confidence.

Watch out!

The key to staying safe is to learn to spot potential hazards and find a route through them. Here are some dangers you may encounter.

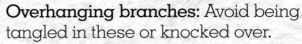

Overhanging branches: Avoid being tangled in these or knocked over.

Fallen tree: This is called a strainer. Water strains through the branches, but you'll be trapped.

Low bridge: Watch your head!

Slippery muddy bank

Rapids

Strong current

Dam

Steep bank

Hole: This is water that sucks backward as it goes over an object underwater.

Waterfall

Rocks and boulders

EXTREME BUT TRUE Large holes (also called stoppers) can be so powerful they may pull you in and under the water.

SMART THINKING

Whitewater paddling always involves risk, but you can avoid many disasters by planning and preparing well.

Plan river trips carefully, finding a route that avoids hazards such as rocks and strong currents.

Pack properly

A good survival kit could save your life. Carry a map, **compass**, and **GPS** so you don't get lost, or to help you find land if you're swept off course. Take a whistle and signal flares to attract attention in an emergency, plus a first aid kit. A **throw-line** can be passed to someone in difficulty and used to tow them to safety.

Watch the weather

Check the weather before setting out. Heavy rain turns rivers into raging torrents, melting snow can cause sudden floods, while storms at sea may whip up enormous waves. Hot weather causes sunburn, and severe cold can chill you to the bone.

Keep an eye on the sky. If dark clouds are gathering, it may be time to stop and make camp. Don't wait until a storm breaks!

THRILL SEEKER

Aleksander Doba (Poland)

FEAT

Longest ever solo kayaking voyage

WHERE AND WHEN

Atlantic Ocean, from Senegal to Brazil, 2010

FAST AND FURIOUS

Many of the strongest, fittest paddlers take part in thrilling races. They may skim along calm water at high speed or twist and turn down stomach-churning rapids.

Speedy slaloms

The most exciting whitewater events are slaloms. Racers hurtle down a 984-foot (300-m) course, weaving in and out of gates, aiming to cross the finish line first. Slaloms are an Olympic event and there are also world slalom championships.

Competitors in the 2013 Canoe Slalom World Cup attempt the specially made course.

Crazy competitions

Other events include freestyle kayaking (performing amazing acrobatic spins, flips, and turns), **kayak polo**, kayak surfing on waves, and canoe sailing (in which small canoes propelled by large sails slice through the water).

THRILL SEEKER

Bridgitte Hartley (South Africa)

FEAT
Women's 1640-feet (500-m) kayak sprint record: 1 minute 46.906 seconds

WHERE AND WHEN
Hungary, 2011

EXTREME BUT TRUE In the Quebec ice canoe race, in Canada, teams of five compete to cross the icy St. Lawrence river.

Teams in Quebec's ice race have to push their boats across thick ice!

19

ENDURANCE TESTS

Some canoers and kayakers love the freedom to travel long distances over open oceans or remote rivers, testing themselves to the limit with hours of paddling.

Out at sea

Sea kayaking is a wonderful way of exploring far-off caves and hidden beaches. Sea kayaks are large, with room for supplies including tents and a cooker. Paddling across vast seas is exhausting, so kayakers travel in groups and tow anyone too tired to go on.

Mighty marathons

Canoe and kayak marathons are usually 19–25 miles (30–40 km), run over several days. They include **portages**, in which racers carry their boats across land. They do this to avoid obstacles such as waterfalls or to get from one stretch of water to another.

Short sea-kayaking trips give you wonderful views of beautiful coastlines.

THRILL SEEKER
Paul Wycherly (Britain)
FEAT
Fastest English Channel crossing by kayak: 2 hours 28 minutes
WHERE AND WHEN
English Channel, 2011

These paddlers are following the curves of a huge river. It's a great way to travel!

EXTREME BUT TRUE The grueling Au Sable River International Canoe Marathon in Michigan is the longest nonstop, two-person canoe race in America. Racers start at 9 p.m. and paddle through the night, finishing 14–19 hours later.

GLOSSARY

blade
The wide, flat end of an oar.

capsize
To turn upside down in a boat on a river or at sea.

compass
A piece of equipment with a magnetic needle that points north. A compass is essential for reading a map or working out which direction you're heading in.

current
Water moving in a certain direction. River currents are strongest in deep, narrow stretches.

dam
A low barrier built across a river to slow the flow of water. Dams are dangerous as they create strong currents that can pull you under.

GPS
A device that picks up signals from satellites in space and uses them to calculate its exact position on the Earth's surface. GPS stands for Global Positioning System.

hull
The main body of a boat, including the bottom and sides.

hypothermia
A very dangerous condition in which someone's body becomes so cold that it stops working properly. Without medical help, they may die.

kayak polo
A fast-moving ball game played on water in lightweight kayaks. Teams try to score in nets, throwing the ball to each other or flicking it with their paddles.

kayak polo

throw-line

portage
Carrying a boat over land to avoid obstacles, or to find water. Many long-distance boat routes have specially made portage trails in sections where the river is too narrow or dangerous.

rapids
Part of a river where the water moves very fast because of a steep, sudden slope in the river bed.

shaft
The handle of a paddle.

throw-line
A long, strong rope (usually stored in a waterproof bag) to throw to another canoeist or kayaker in trouble. It could save someone's life, so make sure you always carry one.

whitewater
Churning, frothy water formed in rapids, where the current becomes fast and unsteady.

shaft

WEBSITES

www.canoeicf.com
Learn about the International Canoe Federation and their exciting program of events.

www.americancanoe.org
Find out about nearby paddling clubs, trails, and competitions.

www.canoekayak.com
Read useful canoeing and kayaking advice and watch videos of epic paddling adventures.

INDEX